GREEN FILES

THIRSTY WORLD

GREEN FILES – THIRSTY WORLD
was produced by

David West 🏃 Children's Books
7 Princeton Court
55 Felsham Road
London SW15 1AZ

Editor: Gail Bushnell
Picture Research: Carlotta Cooper

First published in Great Britain by Heinemann
Library, Halley Court, Jordan Hill, Oxford
OX2 8EJ, part of Harcourt Education.
Heinemann is a registered trademark
of Harcourt Education Ltd.

07 06 05 04 03
10 9 8 7 6 5 4 3 2 1

ISBN 0 431 18292 2 (HB)
ISBN 0 431 18299 X (PB)

British Library Cataloguing in Publication Data

Parker, Steve
Thirsty world. - (Green Files)
1. Water-supply - Juvenile literature
I. Title
333.9'1

PHOTO CREDITS :
Abbreviations: t-top, m-middle, b-bottom, r-right,
l-left, c-centre.

Front cover, mr & 26bl - Corbis Images. Pages 3 &
27br (Philip Dunn); 4-5, 11bl, 24t, 25m (Sipa Press);
9tl (Fotex Medien Agentur GmbH); 13t (Marius
Alexander); 13b (Scott Nelson); 14 (Times
Newspapers Ltd); 21t (John Powell); 21b (Peter
Brooker); 24b (Prinsloo); 28br (Ponopresse
Internationale); 7b, 12-13t, 15t, 18t - Rex Features
Ltd. 4t, 5b, 10-11, 12b & 26br, 19b, 22-23, 23t &
m, 25b (Mark Edwards); 5t (Gilles Corniere); 6b (Jim
Wark); 10 (Dylan Garcia); 11t, 25t, 28bl (Gil Moti),
11br (Jorgen Schytte); 12-13b (Herbert Giradet); 14-
15 (Glen Christian); 16l (Claes Lofgren); 16r (Ron
Giling); 18b (Massimo Lupidi); 19tl (Andre
Maslennikov); 19tr (Alex S. Maclean); 20 (Peter
Arnold); 20-21 (Hartmut Schwarzbach); 22 (Paul
Harrison); 23b (Reinhard Janke); 27t (Paul Howell/
UNEP); 27m (Joerg Boethling); 28-29 (Bojan Brecelj)
- Still Pictures. 6t, 7t, 8t, 9tm, 9b, 16-17, 17 all, 26t,
30 - Corbis Images.

All the Internet addresses (URLs) given in this book
were valid at the time of going to press. However, due
to the dynamic nature of the Internet, some addresses
may have changed, or sites may have ceased to exist
since publication. While the author and publishers
regret any inconvenience this may cause readers, no
responsibility for any such changes can be accepted
by either the author or the publishers.

Printed and bound in Italy

*An explanation of difficult words can be
found in the glossary on page 31.*

GREEN FILES

THIRSTY WORLD

Steve Parker

Heinemann
LIBRARY

CONTENTS

6 THE WATER CYCLE

8 OUR BLUE PLANET

10 WATER SOURCES

12 TRANSPORTING WATER

14 WATER AT HOME

16 HIDDEN USES OF WATER

18 DIRTY WATER

20 SAFE TO DRINK

22 WATER TREATMENT

24 TOO MUCH WATER

26 TOO LITTLE WATER

28 ALTERNATIVE WATER

30 A WATERY FUTURE?

31 GLOSSARY

32 INDEX

The driest places are deserts, and they are spreading fast. This is partly due to climate change as patterns of rainfall alter. It also happens when too many crops are grown and use up the soil's nutrients. The soil turns to sand which lets water soak away.

INTRODUCTION

It has no shape, colour or smell, and when pure, no taste either. We can see right through it and often hardly notice it. Yet, apart from air, it's the single most important substance for our survival. Indeed all living things, from worms to whales, need regular supplies of it. But there are many problems with it. Some places have far too much and are awash with floods. Other places with too little are barren and lifeless. Much of it is dirty and germ-ridden and spreads disease. We can't live without water, so shouldn't we look after it better?

Water pollution is a massive problem. Not only does it kill fish and other wildlife, it also contaminates our own supplies.

Many of the rich, industrialized countries have more than enough water. They are able to waste vast amounts without worrying (left). But for poor, developing countries in dry regions (right), water is far from plentiful. It's a vital, scarce and precious resource that takes much time and effort to obtain.

POWERED BY THE SUN

Water is hardly ever made or destroyed. The same water has been around on Earth for millions of years. And it moves around, too, on a never-ending variety of never-ending journeys called the water cycle.

SOLAR POWER

The movement of water is driven by the heat of the Sun. This warmth, called solar infra-red radiation, makes liquid water 'disappear'. In fact the liquid water changes into a gas, water vapour. We see this when puddles 'dry out' in the sun.

The water cycle is powered by heat energy from the Sun. It warms or evaporates water into invisible water vapour, which rises into the air. However air soon becomes cooler with height.

Water frozen as ice in polar ice-caps, glaciers and on mountains, is still on the move – but very slowly.

Water flows back to the sea in streams and rivers.

Water returns to the surface by gravity. Droplets in clouds clump together and become heavier until pulled down to fall as rain.

Sun's heat evaporates water as vapour from seas and oceans.

Water vapour given off by plants and animals

So the water vapour condenses, or turns back into liquid, as tiny drops – clouds. The larger drops fall as rain, or frozen as sleet, hail or snow. All these forms of water are called precipitation.

Water vapour condenses into droplets in clouds and eventually falls as rain and snow.

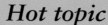

Hot topic

In Peru's mountains, rain and melted snow provided gushing rivers for hydroelectric power. But global warming (due to greenhouse gases trapping heat from the Sun) may mean less rain and snow. Power stations could end up river-less.

Melting snow supplies lowland rivers.

Water seeps into soil and rocks, flows along, and may return to the surface as lakes.

Sun's heat evaporates water from lakes and rivers.

ROUND AND ROUND

Most water turns into water vapour at the surfaces of seas and oceans. But only the water itself does this. The salts it contains in dissolved form are left behind. So the seas remain salty while the pure water vapour rises into the air. It cools as it gets higher in the winds, and turns back into liquid water. This returns to the surface mainly as rain, which flows into streams and rivers, down to the sea – and the cycle continues.

The fresh water we see at the surface is only a tiny amount, compared to the water soaked into the rocks and flowing in underground rivers and lakes.

What water is used for

70% Farm crops and animals

Seen from space, planet 'Earth' is mostly covered by water. But nearly all of this is salty water in seas and oceans.

FRESH, NOT SALTY

Salt water is undrinkable, and would kill our farm crops and animals. We need supplies of fresh water, which has very few salts and other minerals dissolved in it.

EARTH'S WATER RESOURCES

Our planet has plenty of water. Its volume is about 1,320 million cubic kilometres, it makes up 0.2% ($1/500$) of the Earth's total weight, and it covers 70% of its surface. However, only 0.01% ($1/10,000$) of all this water is in the form of liquid fresh water at the surface, in lakes and rivers, or in the air. This is called available fresh water, meaning it is available for us to use.

Salt water 97.5%

97.5% of Earth's water is salty, in seas, oceans, salty lakes, marshes and lagoons.

Fresh water 2.5%

Almost **30%** of fresh water is underground.

Over **70%** of fresh water is frozen as ice.

Available fresh water 0.01%

68.2% of liquid surface water is in lakes and rivers.

Less than **1.6%** is in plants and animals.

About **8.5%** is in soils.

About **12.2%** is in swamps, marshes and wetlands.

About **9.5%** is water vapour and clouds in the air.

9% Domestic

21% Industrial

HOW WE USE WATER

The water which comes out of our taps is only a tiny amount of all the water we use. Most is led along channels, pipes and ditches to irrigate farm crops in fields and glasshouses. Water is also provided for farm animals to drink and to clean their living places. These agricultural uses account for more than two-thirds of all water used around the world. Another one-fifth of this water is supplied to factories and industrial sites like paper-mills and chemical works.

Water spins fan-like turbines to turn generators and make electricity. This use of water provides almost one-fifth of all the world's electricity.

Hot topic

In desert regions, water is in short supply for all uses. It's especially difficult to grow crops in dry soil. Most years, the majority of people just manage. But in drought years, millions may die.

No water = no food.

9

Even the driest deserts have some water. But it is usually deep under the ground. To obtain it, people have to dig or drill deep. It's easier to use water at the surface.

WATER'S ROLE IN HISTORY

Easily available surface water has had a huge effect on world history. Most towns and cities grew up on the banks of rivers or lakes, or at estuaries where rivers flow into the sea. Here, fresh water could be used for drinking, cooking, cleaning and crops, to power machines like water-wheels, and as transport routes or 'highways' for ships and boats.

In dry regions the main water sources are aquifers – rocks which are slightly porous and hold groundwater like a 'stony sponge'. These are tapped by drilling shafts called boreholes.

WATER AND LAND

A river is fed by its catchment area. This is where rain, snow and other precipitation fall and collect into streams which join the river. Lakes form where the land dips down into a basin, or behind a wall-like dam.

Dry on top, but water below: wind-powered pumps raise groundwater into large storage tanks. These hold enough to last for weeks without wind.

Reservoir behind dam

Low-land lake

Meltwater lake

Crater lake in old volcano

Desert river

Oasis

Fault

Hot topic

A dam is a wall across a river. It holds back water to form a reservoir (artificial lake). The stored water has many uses. But as the reservoir fills, it may flood homes, farms and even whole towns. People must be moved to new houses on higher ground.

Waters rise, Sardah Dam, India.

ROCKS AND WATER

The way that water flows and collects is greatly affected by the rocks at or just under the surface. If they are porous (permeable), water can slowly soak in and continue moving underground. Non-porous rocks do not allow this. Water flows over them into streams and smaller rivers (tributaries), which merge into the main river.

Some rain soaks into porous rock and flows underground. The level below which the rock is saturated or 'full' of water is called the water table.

Non-porous rock

Porous rock

Water table level

Saturated rock

Oases are pools of water in deserts. They may form where underground water oozes up faults or cracks in the rocks.

Raising or pumping up water from wells and boreholes needs energy. This can come from wind (opposite), engines, motors – or muscle power.

11

Water is difficult to transport. It's heavy and bulky, it splashes and sloshes, and it leaks from any tiny crack or hole. But it has one useful feature – it flows.

HEAVY DEMAND

In most places water must be moved from its sources, like rivers, lakes, wells and reservoirs, to where it's needed. One method is to use water containers, from large trucks and tankers to barrels and buckets. But this takes much time and uses up great energy and effort.

In some countries, safe drinking water comes by special tanker. Ordinary tap water is less safe.

Cities like London have water supply pipes below ground, which are emptied for repair (above).

Open channels let water get dirty and evaporate. Pipes keep it clean and reduce loss (below).

Go with the flow
Most developed countries have mains water supplies with channels, pipes, tubes and ducts. Water moves along by the force of gravity. In places it must be raised, usually by motorized pumps, so it flows down again and onwards.

In poor areas, collecting water from a shared tap or well is a vital, time-consuming daily job. All family members take a turn.

13

We turn on the tap, and clean water comes out, safe for drinking and cooking. But for two billion people around the world, this 'luxury' is a distant dream.

WHERE WATER GOES

The most important use of water is for drinking, on its own or in squash, coffee and so on. But this makes up less than one-hundredth of what we use at home. Some people suggest two supplies – one clean and pure, and one less so for utility jobs (below), which would be much cheaper to provide.

HOUSEHOLD WATER USE

Working 29%

Drinking 1%

Utility 70%

Drinking water includes water for cooking. Working water is used to wash ourselves, our clothes and dishes. Utility water is for general cleaning, car-washing, heating systems, houseplants and gardens.

When water is scarce and takes time and effort to obtain, hauling it up from a local well, people are much more careful about how they use it.

Many countries charge people for water by the volume they use, measured by a meter. This helps people to be aware of water's worth and always save it.

Being GREEN
To wash the car or water the plants, it's easy to turn on a garden tap. Yet it's almost as easy to fit a water barrel or butt to collect rain, and use this instead. It's far cheaper and better for the environment too. *Money down the drain!*

SENSIBLE SAVINGS

Everyone can save precious water. A bath takes 80–100 litres, a shower one-third of this. A standard flush toilet uses 15 litres, a quick-flush one almost half this amount. A dripping tap can waste a litre every hour. 'Economy' settings on washing machines and dishwashers also bring great savings.

HOW MUCH WATER PER PERSON?

Each day at home, a person in a developed country such as the USA uses 12 times more water than someone from a developing country. Every drop costs money, time and energy to purify for use and treat after use, and reduces the amount of available fresh water.

Africa
47 litres/day

Asia
85 litres/day

Europe
334 litres/day

USA
578 litres/day

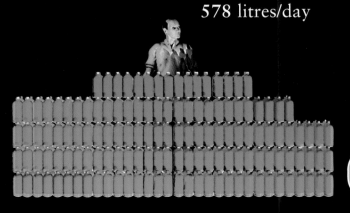

The water we use at home is only a small amount of the water we consume in other ways. Almost everything we buy, eat, sit on, wear, travel in and switch on needed water.

TEN TIMES MORE

Every product and item requires water to manufacture, from obtaining raw materials, to making the machines at the factory, to transporting finished goods to the shops. We do not see these 'hidden' uses, but they increase our personal use up to ten times.

Electricity for one hour of TV 500 litres

Power stations need water to cool the high-temperature, high-pressure steam that spins their generators. They are usually built near rivers or the sea.

One newspaper 30 litres

Making paper, card and board uses huge amounts of water. One copy of a small newspaper represents 30 litres. For a thick weekend newspaper with magazines, this rises to 200.

A shiny new car does not seem very watery. But all the materials and processes used to manufacture it (below) take up precious water.

One drinks can 100 litres

A drinks can of the metal aluminium holds about one-third of a litre – but making it uses 300 times more water.

One car 500,000 litres

HOW MUCH IS LOTS?

It may be difficult to imagine such huge amounts of water. A person in a developed country is responsible, every day, for over 1,000 litres, which weighs one tonne – more than a typical family car. In fact, to make such a car uses half a million litres, enough to fill a fairly large swimming pool.

Hot topic

The food industry is one of the biggest consumers of water. It's used to irrigate crops, provide for animals, and wash all produce ready for sale. To make prepared, processed convenience foods, the amounts leap up five or ten times. A ready-washed, bagged-up salad could mean a dustbin-full of water.

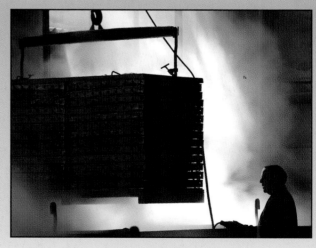

Softening tuna fish by steaming.

Water from our taps is usually safe. But what about water from a dirty brown puddle or a frothy yellow river? It may harbour germs, chemicals and poisons – but then, so might clear, sparkling water.

LOOKS CAN LIE

Many substances dissolve and 'disappear' into water without trace. We cannot see them because water is such a good solvent. Yet clear water that looks pure could be swarming with germs and full of toxins. About one-third of the people in the world lack safe drinking water.

Dead fish litter the banks of the River Seine, Paris, France – result of a chemical spill.

A clean river in Italy suddenly became a flowing ribbon of foam. The disaster was due to chemicals from a local factory which, under local laws, were allowed to pour into the water.

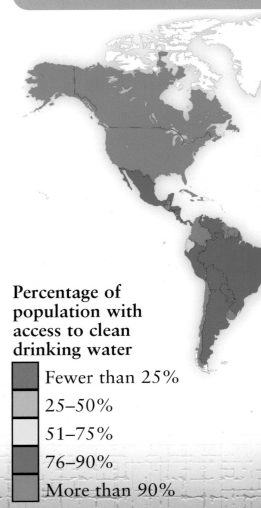

Percentage of population with access to clean drinking water

Fewer than 25%

25–50%

51–75%

76–90%

More than 90%

Water may not be safe even when it falls from the sky. These trees are dying from acid rain.

Hot topic

Nutrients in water feed living things. But too many nutrients from fertilizers or sewage mean that microbes which are usually rare, breed out of control. This upsets nature's balance and causes toxic 'tides' that harm wildlife.

Algal tide, Lake Eyrie, USA.

SAFE DRINKING WATER

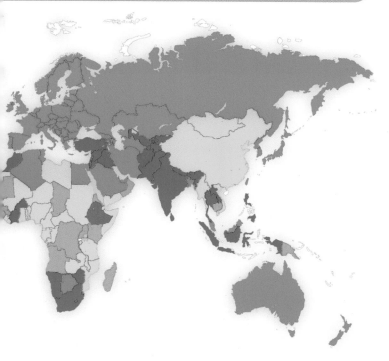

People in rich industrialized countries take clean, pure water for granted. But more than two billion people have little or no access to safe water for drinking and cooking. The most affected countries are in Africa, especially south of the Sahara Desert, where even dirty water is scarce.

GLOBAL CONCERN

In 2002, world leaders held an Earth Summit in Johannesburg, South Africa. A major aim was to provide clean water for more people to reduce spread of disease. Sadly there was no clear agreement.

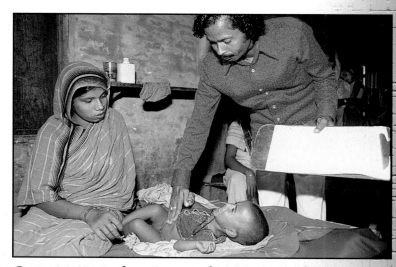

Contaminated water is the source of many deadly diseases such as cholera, dysentery and typhoid. They kill three million people yearly.

19

Treating water to make it clean and pure, safe for drinking and cooking, is both a complicated technical process and a massive business.

NATURALLY PURE

In general, water from wells, boreholes and other sources deep in the ground is cleaner than surface water in lakes and rivers. As the water soaks slowly through the rocks, germs and impurities are removed. Water supply plants use the same process by making water flow slowly through filter beds of gravel and sand.

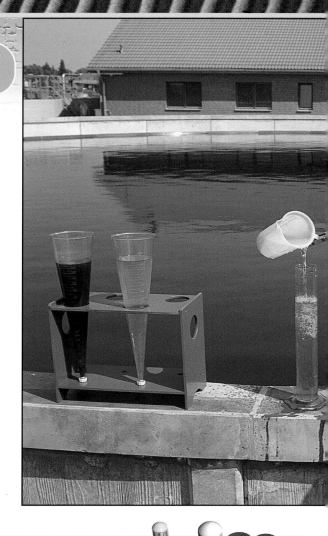

Water sources, especially rivers, are checked often. In a dry summer there are more natural impurities.

CLEANING WATER

The water supply system cleans water in several stages. Chemicals added in coagulation tanks cause certain impurities to clump together and settle to the bottom. The water trickles into layers of gravel, then sand, which remove more impurities. Added disinfectant chemicals kill any remaining germs before storage.

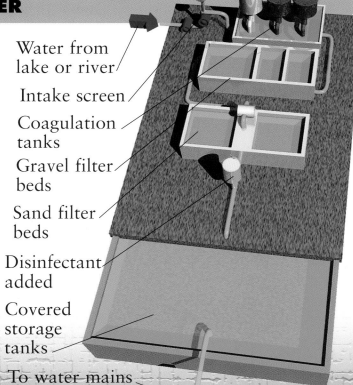

Water from lake or river

Intake screen

Coagulation tanks

Gravel filter beds

Sand filter beds

Disinfectant added

Covered storage tanks

To water mains

Samples of water are taken regularly and tested for levels of harmful chemicals and germs. The amounts of purifying chemicals can be varied, depending on the source, like a well or river.

ADDED CHEMICALS

Several chemicals are added to the water in exact amounts. For example activated carbon absorbs impurities which may not be harmful, but which would give the water an unpleasant taste or smell. Chlorine is also bubbled through the water to help kill germs. Greater amounts of chlorine chemicals in swimming pools give them their distinctive odour.

Hot topic

In many regions, one of the chemicals added to water, as a public health measure, is fluoride. This does not affect the quality of the water itself, but it does affect our well-being. Tiny amounts of fluoride help our teeth to stay strong and healthy.

Some toothpastes have extra fluoride.

Tiny amounts of minerals give different sources of water their own tastes. This is especially noticeable in bottled water.

WATER TREATMENT

Used water that flows away down the plug-hole, drain or toilet does not simply 'disappear'. It enters a complicated cleaning process at the local water treatment plant.

READY FOR RELEASE

At the treatment plant, all kinds of solids and chemicals are removed in a step-by-step process. The aim is to make the water clean enough to flow back into nature, usually into a river or lake.

Reedbeds and marshes are being increasingly used to clean water naturally. The plants' roots filter the water and use nutrients for growth.

Half the world's people do not have flushing toilets. They use pit latrines or even simple holes in the ground, filling them in and changing site every few days.

SEWAGE

At the treatment plant, used or 'foul' water (1) is screened to remove large solids (2). It stands in sedimentation beds (3) where small particles settle out as sludge. 'Friendly' bacteria and other microbes breeding in the biological beds (4) are used to kill and remove harmful microbes. This process continues as water trickles from rotating booms in the circular wetbeds (5). The cleaned water flows into a local river (6) while sludge and other leftovers are put into digestion tanks (7). Here they rot and give off the gas methane, which is burned to generate electricity in a power station (8). The final sludge remnants are taken away by road, rail (9) or ship (10) for use as fertilizer.

Being GREEN

New, better methods of water treatment are always being tested. In membrane filtration, waste water is passed through a special sheet-like membrane to remove impurities. The system is fast to set up and costs less than a full-scale plant, and is suitable for smaller amounts of water.

Membrane filtration.

USED MANY TIMES

Along rivers with many towns and cities, it is estimated that the same water is taken out, used, cleaned and put back in, perhaps six or seven times. The by-products of water treatment include sludges and slurries with many minerals and nutrients. These are allowed to decay or 'digest' and produce methane gas, to burn for heat or power.

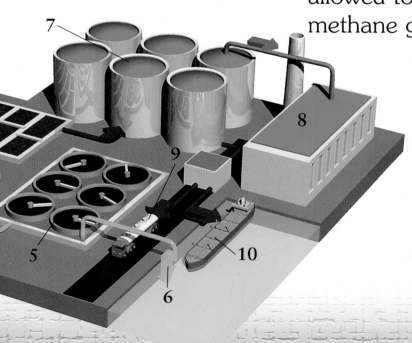

Sludges and slurries from water treatment plants or sewage works are spread on the land as fertilizer, but only after all harmful microbes and chemicals are removed.

Each year, on average, water kills up to 1,000 people – not by carrying germs and disease, but by drowning them in floods. The problem of global warming (see page 7), leading to climate change, could make this terrible toll rise.

STORMS AND FLOODS

For thousands of years, most places have coped with their natural amounts of rain and other forms of water. They have rivers and lakes big enough to hold sudden downpours such as tropical monsoon storms.

Scientific studies show that storms are becoming more common and powerful around the world. Heavy rain in upland areas causes rivers to burst their banks, as here in France, 2002.

In 2000, floods covered vast areas of Mozambique, Africa. The waters destroyed buildings, crops, roads and electricity supplies and ruined farmland.

Cutting down trees increases flooding. Without tree roots to hold the soil, it is washed by rain into rivers, where it clogs the channels. Water cannot pass and spills over the land.

CHANGING CLIMATE

Air pollution by 'greenhouse gases' is predicted to make world temperatures rise. The gases trap heat in the atmosphere in the same way that glass traps heat in a greenhouse. As a result, some places will not only be warmer, but wetter, as patterns of rainfall alter and storms increase. This could lead to devastating floods.

Hot topic

Floods which occur regularly can be useful. In parts of China and Egypt, flooding rivers spread nourishing silt on the land, in which farm crops then thrive. But new dams and irrigation schemes are disrupting these age-old occurrences.

Flood defences, North China.

London's Thames River Barrier is a series of 'gates' which can be lifted to prevent very high tides flooding the city. But as sea levels rise with global warming, the barrier may be unable to cope.

25

Deserts are the driest places, receiving less than 15 centimetres of rain each year. Yet some plants, animals and even people survive there, suited to conserving water and using it sparingly. Sadly, too many people with modern lifestyles have not adapted in the same way.

OASIS IN THE DESERT

Wildlife fits in with its environment. People do the opposite – we change our surroundings to suit ourselves. In places where water is scarce, people are using it thousands of times faster than it can be replenished naturally. Even where water is plentiful, in some big cities more than half is lost as leaks and seepages.

Hot topic

On the USA's Colorado River, dams like Glen Canyon and many irrigation pipes reduce the water flow by up to nine-tenths. The habitat for wildlife is so altered, fish like humpback chub (which live only here) are in danger of extinction.

Glen Canyon dam.

North America
The Great Lakes hold one-fifth of the world's surface fresh water. But average levels have fallen a metre in 30 years.

Where water is scarce

■ High population

□ Low population

Central America
Mexico City was once a maze of channels and lakes. So much water has been taken from under the ground that parts of the city have sunk eight metres in 100 years.

SUCKING THE ROCKS DRY

The greatest use for water in dry regions is to irrigate crops. People also want green lawns, wooded parks, swimming pools, fountains and golf courses. Water for these is raised from boreholes and wells. Such use is not sustainable, as rocks take thousands of years to collect water and many boreholes run dry in less than ten years.

Aral Sea
So much water has been taken from this inland lake, for farms and industry, that its area has halved in 50 years.

China
The gigantic Three Gorges hydroelectric project on the Ch'ang Jiang (Yangtze) River could mean this waterway is dry downstream in summer.

Africa
South of the Sahara, the Sahel area has suffered years of droughts, combined with trying to grow too many crops. The soil turns to desert sand.

India
Each monsoon season brings up to 10 metres of rain. But so many farms and people use it faster than it can fall.

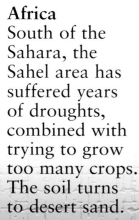

27

Main methods of dealing with water, like boreholes, dams, pipes, pumps, purifying it before use and treating it after, have been much the same for many years. Can any newer technologies help the water crisis?

Desalination is very expensive, both when constructing the pipes, tanks and machines, and in running costs.

WATER FROM AIR

Some places have little surface water but plenty just above, as fog and mist. In fog collection, large mesh-like sheets are held between tall poles in the drifting fog. Tiny drops gather and merge to make bigger ones that drip into a channel below.

Hot topic

Polar ice is made of highly squeezed snow. It melts to give relatively pure water. Suitable-sized icebergs can be located by satellite photographs, hitched by cables and then towed by boat to warmer regions, where the melting water is collected.

Fog collection was pioneered in Chungungo, a remote village in Chile. Almost 100 collectors gather an average of 40 litres of water for each person every day. Before this, the amount available was 15 litres.

A captured berg near Greenland.

FRESH WATER FROM SALTY

When the Sun warms the sea, water vapour evaporates and then condenses as it cools into pure water. This process is copied in desalination, or 'de-salting'. Sea water is heated in huge pipes or towers, and the water vapour is captured and condensed into clean, fresh water. Supplies of salty water for this process are almost limitless. But the energy and raw materials needed to build the equipment and heat the water make it costly. Desalination is helpful where desert lands meet the sea and energy, such as petroleum, is plentiful.

COULD WE MAKE RAIN?

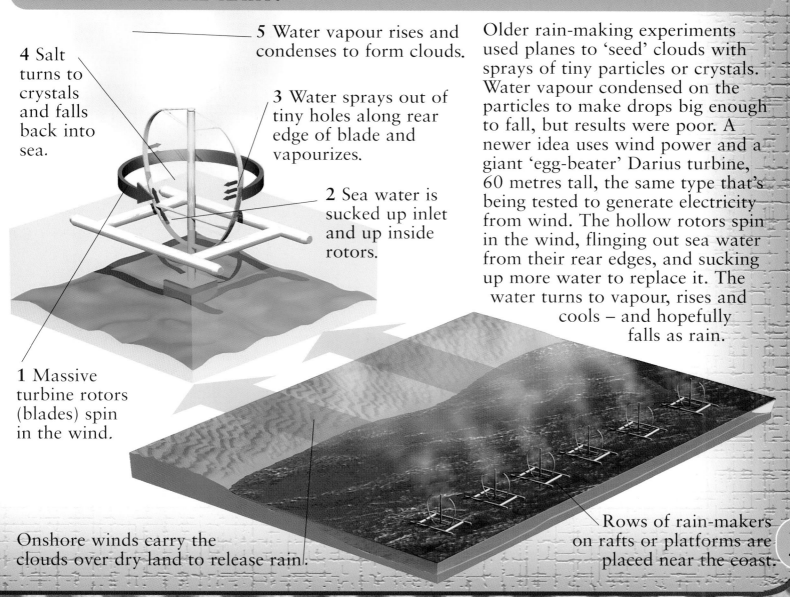

5 Water vapour rises and condenses to form clouds.

4 Salt turns to crystals and falls back into sea.

3 Water sprays out of tiny holes along rear edge of blade and vapourizes.

2 Sea water is sucked up inlet and up inside rotors.

1 Massive turbine rotors (blades) spin in the wind.

Older rain-making experiments used planes to 'seed' clouds with sprays of tiny particles or crystals. Water vapour condensed on the particles to make drops big enough to fall, but results were poor. A newer idea uses wind power and a giant 'egg-beater' Darius turbine, 60 metres tall, the same type that's being tested to generate electricity from wind. The hollow rotors spin in the wind, flinging out sea water from their rear edges, and sucking up more water to replace it. The water turns to vapour, rises and cools – and hopefully falls as rain.

Onshore winds carry the clouds over dry land to release rain.

Rows of rain-makers on rafts or platforms are placed near the coast.

The world is getting thirstier, as people use more water. In 30 years, half of all people – more than three billion – could face drastic shortages as supplies run out.

GREEN WATER

Today, billions must make do with dirty water to wash, cook and drink. Waterborne diseases kill six people every minute. Wars have been fought over areas that are rich in water. Even you can do something about cutting down on water wastage. Choose showers over baths, turn taps off and maybe make a poster to encourage others to do the same.

Addresses and websites for further information

WATERAID
Prince Consort House,
27-29 Albert Embankment,
London,
SE1 7UB
Tel 020 7793 4500
www.wateraid.org.uk/
Major charity who aim to provide safe domestic water and hygiene education to the world's poorest people.

'WATERWISE' SCHEMES
Organized by water utilities and companies, such as:
Thames Water Utilities Ltd,
PO Box 436,
Swindon,
SN38 1TU
www.thames-water.com/waterwise/
Useful tips for saving water.

SAVE WATER AT HOME
www.environment-agency.gov.uk/subjects/waterres
Run by the Environmental Agency with top tips for saving water in the home.

AUSTRALIAN GREENHOUSE OFFICE
GPO Box 621,
Canberra ACT 2601,
Australia
Tel 1800 130 606
Fax 02 9274 1390
www.greenhouse.gov.au

FRIENDS OF THE EARTH
26-28 Underwood Street,
London,
N1 7JQ
Tel 020 7490 1555
Fax 020 7490 0881
www.foe.co.uk
International network of groups. For the conservation of water resources and provision of clean water for people worldwide.

GREENPEACE UK
Canonbury Villas,
London,
N1 2PN
Tel 020 7865 8100
Fax 020 7865 8200
E-mail
info@uk.greenpeace.org
www.greenpeace.org.uk
Campaigning organization. Support water conservation and clean water supplies.

www.sally-save-water.com/
Website full of information.

ENVIRONMENT PROTECTION AUTHORITY
Environment Australia,
GPO Box 787,
Canberra ACT 2601,
Australia
Tel 02 6274 1111
Fax 02 6274 1666
www.environment.gov.au

GLOSSARY

catchment area
The area of land which gathers rain and other forms of precipitation for a river.

condense
When the gas called water vapour cools and turns into liquid water.

drought
A long period with little or no rain or other precipitation.

evaporate
When liquid water is heated and turns into a gas called water vapour.

hydroelectricity
Electrical power generated from the energy of running water, usually by a power station at a dam built across a river.

irrigate
To bring water from a river, lake, well or other source, usually to supply crops and other plants.

oasis
A small place in the desert which has water, usually seeping up from under the ground. Plants grow and animals and people come to drink.

porous
A substance which has tiny holes, like a bath sponge or certain kinds of rock, allowing water to slowly soak in and flow along.

precipitation
All forms of water that reach the ground from the air, including rain, hail, sleet, snow, dew, fog, mist and frost.

reservoir
An artificial or man-made lake, usually where water piles up in the river valley behind a dam.

water vapour
Water in the form of a gas, which is invisible and mixes with the other gases in air.

acid rain 19
aquifers 10

baths 15, 30
boats 10
bottled water 21

carbon, activated 21
chemicals 18, 20,
    21, 22
chlorine 21
climate change 4, 24
clouds 6, 7, 29

desalination 28, 29
disease 5, 19, 30
drinking water 10,
    12, 14, 18,
    19, 20, 30
drought 9, 27, 31

electricity 7, 9, 16,
    22, 27, 31

fish 5, 18, 26
floods 5, 24–25
fog 28, 31
fresh water 7, 8,
    10, 26, 29

germs 5, 18 , 20, 21
glaciers 6
Glen Canyon dam 26
global warming 7, 24
greenhouse gases 25

ice 6, 8, 28
industry 9, 16, 27
irrigation 9, 17, 25,
    26, 27, 31

mist 28, 31
monsoon rain 24, 27

newspapers 16

oases 10, 11, 26, 31
oceans 6, 7, 8

plants 6, 8, 26
pollution 5, 25
precipitation 7, 10, 31

rain making 29
reservoirs 10, 11,
    12, 31

salty water 7, 8, 29
sea 6, 7, 8, 29

sewage 19, 22, 23
ships 10
showers 15
snow 7, 10, 28, 31
soil 4, 7, 25, 27
storms 24, 25
streams 6, 7
Sun 6, 7

tap water 9, 12, 14,
    18, 30
Thames Barrier 25
Three Gorges 27
toxic tides 19

underground water
    7, 8, 10, 11, 13, 26,
    31

water cycle 6–7
water supplies 13, 20
water table 11
water treatment 22–23
water vapour 6, 7,
    29, 31
water wheels 10
wells 11, 12, 14,
    20, 27, 31
wildlife 5, 19, 26